First published in the United States in 1999 by Peter Bedrick Books
A division of NTC/Contemporary Publishing Group, Inc
4255 West Touhy Avemue
Lincolnwood (Chicago), Illinois 60646-1975 U.S.A.

© Macdonald Young Books 1999
Text and illustrations © Alan Baker 1999

Editor: Lisa Edwards
Designer: Celia Hart
Natural History Consultant: Stephen Savage

Library of Congress Cataloging-in-Publication Data is available from the
United States Library of Congress.

Printed and bound in Portugal by Edições ASA

International Standard Book Number: 0-87226-541-2

00 01 02 03 04 05 15 14 13 12 11 10 9 8 7 6 5 4 3 2 1

LOOK WHO LIVES IN...

The Desert

ALAN BAKER

PETER BEDRICK BOOKS
NEW YORK

Down in the dusty, dry desert, something is looking at an ant. It's a scuttling, stinging…

scorpion!
It has two big claws, and a long, curled tail. Clambering over a sandy rock, something is looking at the scorpion.
It's a spiny, scaly…

horned lizard!
It has tiny claws and a spiky
back. Chewing on a cactus seed,
something is looking at the
horned lizard.
It's a squeaking, leaping…

kangaroo rat!
It has strong back legs for jumping.
Snoozing sleepily in the shade,
something is looking at the
kangaroo rat.
It's a crawling, croaking...

13

spadefoot toad!
It has soft, moist skin and big, flat
feet. Perched upon a prickly cactus,
something is looking at the
spadefoot toad.
It's a picking, pecking…

woodpecker!
It has a sharp, pointed beak for digging. Basking in the baking sun, something is looking at the woodpecker.
It's a slithering, tail-shaking...

rattlesnake!
It has a rattle on the end of its tail.
Clinging tightly to a boulder,
something is looking at
the rattlesnake.
It's a rushing, racing…

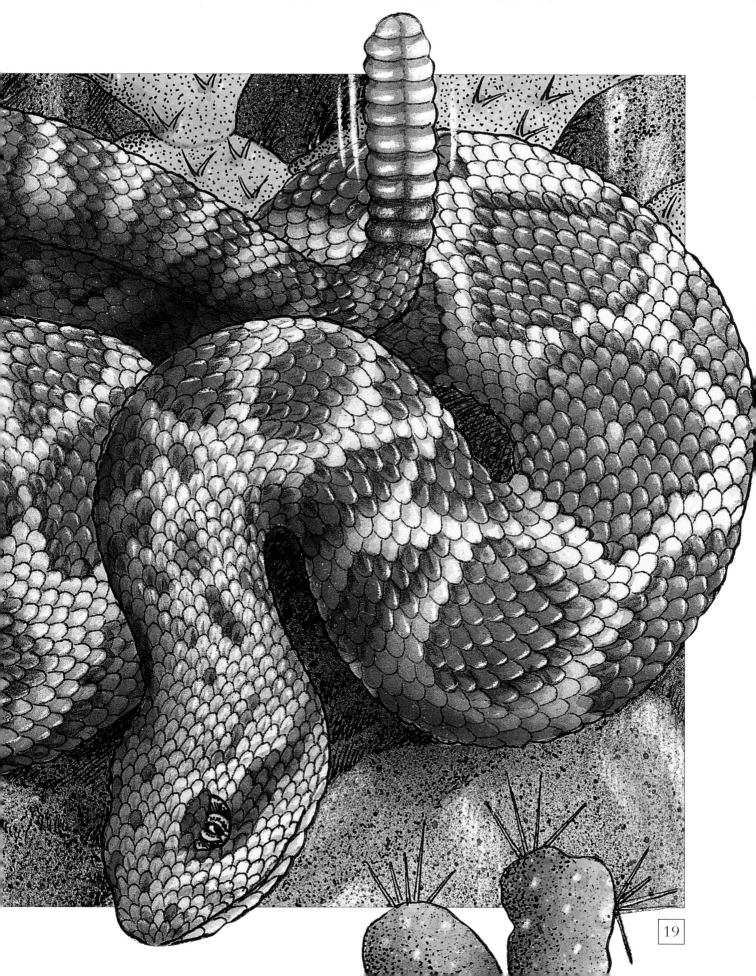

roadrunner!
It has a feathery crest on
its head. Slithering slowly
over a rugged rock, something
is looking at the roadrunner.
It's a creepy, sleepy...

gila monster!
It has brilliant, beady skin.
Sneaking silently across a sandy
stone, something is looking at the
gila monster.
It's a cautious, cunning...

kit fox!
It is very shy and has
large, sensitive ears.
High above on a desert hill,
something is looking at the kit fox.
It's a pouncing, preying…

puma! The puma can see
all of the animals:
the roadrunner, the
kit fox, the gila
monster, the rattlesnake,
the woodpecker,

the spadefoot toad,
the kangaroo rat,
the horned lizard, the
scorpion and the ant.
Can *you* see them all?

The World's Deserts

The map below shows the areas of desert around the world. Deserts are sandy, rocky places which are extremely hot in the daytime and very cold at night. Strong winds often blow for at least part of the year. For months at a time, there is very little water. Then, it may rain so much that plants bloom overnight.

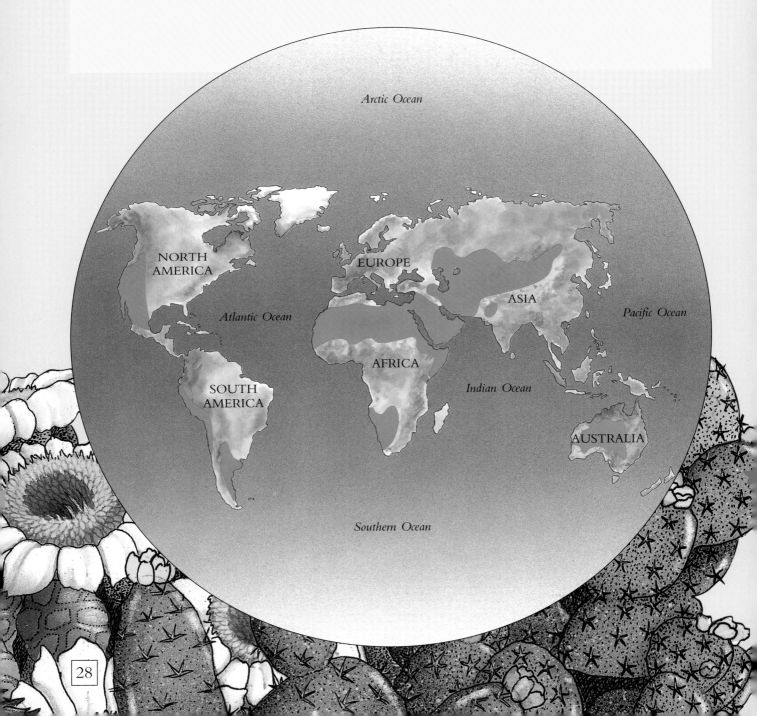

Index

Ant, page 7: Harvester ants gather seeds and store them in huge underground nests 2–3 yards wide. If the seeds become damp, the ants carry them outside to dry.

Gila monster, page 23: Gila monsters are poisonous lizards about 20 inches long. They eat nesting birds, baby mammals, eggs and reptiles.

Horned lizard, page 11: Horned lizards catch insects with their long tongues. They bury themselves up to their necks so that they can watch everything around them.

Kangaroo rat, page 13: Kangaroo rats are able to leap using their powerful back legs. They carry food in their cheek pouches and then store it in burrows.

Kit fox, page 24: Kit foxes like to live in burrows belonging to other animals. They come out at night to hunt lizards, rodents and rabbits.

Puma, page 26: Pumas can grow to 10 feet in length and are extremely powerful. They can leap for a distance of 43 feet and as high as 16 feet.

Rattlesnake, page 19: Diamond-backed rattlesnakes are 3–7 feet long and are highly poisonous. They shake the rattles on their tails to scare other animals.

Roadrunner, page 20: Roadrunners are a type of cuckoo and are about 2 feet long. They run at speeds of up to 29 miles per hour.

Scorpion, page 9: Scorpions like very hot places. Their pincer-like claws are used as tools and weapons. The poisonous sting at the tip of their tails can kill a human.

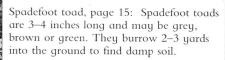
Spadefoot toad, page 15: Spadefoot toads are 3–4 inches long and may be grey, brown or green. They burrow 2–3 yards into the ground to find damp soil.

Woodpecker, page 17: Gilded flicker woodpeckers dig out the soft flesh of giant cacti to make their nests. After their young have left, other birds use the nests.

Desert plants have adapted to a lack of water. Some are able to store water, like cacti. Others have deep roots of 66 feet or more to reach water deep underground. Some plants only live during the rainy season.